The
Uncountability
of Love

The
Uncountability
of Love

Rachna Chowla

The Swirling Leaf Press

The Swirling Leaf Press

www.swirlingleafpress.com
info@swirlingleafpress.com

Book design by Mash Chudasama
www.mash-design.com

Cover image by Catrin Welz-Stein
www.catrinwelzstein.com

Printed in the United Kingdom

First edition printed in 2022

ISBN: 978-0-9957669-1-4

For my dear parents Manju and Yugesh,
and for all my other teachers,
with my uncountable love

Contents

Foreword by Rupert Spira:
'Before There Was Ever a
You or an I'

Rachna does not write poems; she is written by them.

When the self vanishes, the world takes its place. As Li Po said, 'I sit, the mountain and I, until only the mountain remains.' Rachna sits, the paper and her, 'Every dawn spent on an ocean made of paper plain, paper white / My pencil the mast and the spaces between my thoughts the sails to catch the winds....' And her sitting is an invitation that the winds might gather and coalesce into a poem that may take us with it into the world before it was filtered through the prism of thought.

Poetry is not an escape into an imaginary world; it is a portal from the imaginary world in which we move without realising it, into the real world in which we live without seeing it. Each of Rachna's poems is one such portal. We follow her into the eyes of her companion, 'Into the untamed majesty / Of wild, notionless beauty...'; we taste iridescent, iris blue; we become the horizon; our body dissolves in transparency and luminosity; we find our self repeatedly 'arriving at the slow caressed / Cocooning of beingness....'

As Kathleen Raine wrote in her exquisite meditation on the surrender required for truly intimate relationship, 'I am the way to die.' In Rachna's poems we disappear with her again and again. We slip beneath the surface of the world, 'falling / Falling / But what was left to even fall into / Other than falling into us?'

And we find ourself, not on the shore of another world, but in this world, each time as if for the first time. The world is not *what* we see; it is *the way* we see.

Each of Rachna's poems is a love poem into which we, the beloved, are drawn time and again, an invitation that 'vanishes itself and us / Into the magnificence of nothingness / Once its work is done.' We do not *find* ourself there in love; we *lose* ourself in love.

It is out of this love that Rachna's poems blossom.

Rupert Spira
March 2022

First, a little note

This book of poetry has a rather unusual name, one that is based on a mathematical theorem called *The Uncountability of Real Numbers.* I was introduced to it, quite by chance, by my friend Jenny and something about it captured me, *the almost otherworldly beauty about its uncountable infinity,* even though I have never been able to understand its proof.

And even ordinary mathematics expresses something of this extraordinary, *otherworldly* beauty – just the mere existence of the number π (pi), which after its decimal point, has digits that go on, infinitely so. Or the number φ (phi), also known as the *golden ratio* or the *divine proportion* because of its ubiquitous (and miraculous) expression in the natural world through the Fibonacci series appearing deep within the microcosm of what makes up our cells – the DNA helix, or the world we live in – petals, plants, and even in the spiral galaxies of the cosmos. *What sheer elegance and beauty?*

And perhaps this is the same elegance and beauty that I am taken to upon reading the poetic lines of Rumi, *'Lovers don't finally meet somewhere / They're in each other all along.'* Or, *'In the existence of your love, I have become non-existent / This non-existence linked to you is better than all existence.'*

Or when my eyes and heart are captured by a piece of art, or that place I am taken to whenever I fall into the long moonbeam gaze of someone's eyes?

It's as if some forms or experiences have the ability to uncloak themselves, revealing a secret door through which we step into this sense of beauty, or perhaps the uncloaking reveals a mirror instead, into which we gaze and lose ourselves, in eternal moments of our own boundless beauty?

So why, then, *The Uncountability of Love?* Because *Love*, like Truth and Beauty, is not bound by any number, nor by any form, and *coming to know this is joy itself.*

And for sharing this understanding, my forever thanks and uncountable love to my teachers, Rupert Spira & Francis Lucille.

Rachna xx

1.
What I write about when I write about writing

Even after all these years of writing poetry, there remains a delicious mystery about the process of writing – from where the poems arrive and to where they lead. Between me, my page and my pen, I seem to be the last to know anything about the journey that each poem is about to take, as the words start to appear, letter by letter, on the page. It's like some sort of lovely universal conspiracy.

And the poems themselves are wise teachers too. They continue to teach me the Zen art of effortless writing, of being led by their own rhythm, and of a patience best described by Jean Klein as *"waiting without waiting"*. You cannot prize open a bud to hasten its flowering, and it is the same with a poem. They find their own flow, their own form, and their own endings, as and when they wish to do so.

So, in thanks to these poem-teachers of mine and to the mystery, a chapter of poems about poems.

Birth of the musings

The humdrum of busy lands
A shhhh of leaves - time's unmoving sands

A pencil sailing across a page - oh such luxurious tip-tapping
Neurons silently clapping, then pausing, then clapping

A lush-palmed island, an oasis made of me
Inhabited by a pencil, some paper and, of course, serenity

Lapped by azure seas, all that I need
Oh beautiful words, how my soul you nourish and feed

The journey of a poem begins not on Earth, but among the stars
A murmuration of words arriving, felt ours, but not ours

A sanctuary, the world sensed, complete yet moated
Each line a love letter arriving in the post, embraced and noted

Because the pencil's lead at its midnight never knows
What the cosmos will create, and what follows and flows

And that Dear Reader of my oasis thoughts, is the beauty of
poetry and verse

For they form a bridge across the universe, which you and I so
happily traverse.

Take-off

So you came?
I sense your gentle tremulousness inside my chest
A note arriving in my heart
Tip-tapping of fingers between each beat
And this...

Make of it all what you will
But we all know when Love is at one's door
Or when a poem is about to find her wings.

Poems that fly

I could spend all my days with them
With those poems that fly
The encapsulation
Of the dwellings deep in another's heart
A message from somewhere else in time
Or better still
If I am allowed to watch
The words themselves
Drop from the sky
Condensing out from thin air
Onto a sheet
Stark naked
Lily-white
As their blots decide who else to invite
And indeed how they together might sit
And the point to which they point

As much a surprise to my hands, as to your eyes

And the title, well that comes much later

Wondrous they are
These words that paint me into their own imagination.

An ever so nightly sky

Afloat on my blue velvet sofa
My fingers back, writing again
Asking for rain
So that they can tip-tap along
With the rhapsody of everything
And have an excuse to do nothing else
Ah, I have missed this
The simple joy of not knowing
And just watching the words appear
Like stars, in an ever so nightly sky.

Paper boat sailing

Here we meet for the first time and in this particular way
I wonder what conversations we'll share and what you'll say?

Which sutras will you teach? To which depths will we go?
With you whispering me your words and me forever in tow

And what can I offer for these gifts? I don't want to just receive
Is that my ego speaking, that I now perceive?

Whether yes or no, I offer to be like a boat
And be carried with you, to wherever, as we float

Every dawn spent on an ocean made of paper plain, paper white
My pencil the mast and the spaces between my thoughts the sails
to catch the winds, even slight

And every morn we shall be together and see what the winds
have in store
New-found islands of ideas, bejewelled with new fauna and the
imagination's more

And perhaps days caught in the doldrums, the oceans like a desert,
but still we shall share our *amour de la mer*
Together we would simply sit and bob a little too in the non-waiting
waters, and feel the ocean breathe herself into the air

All from the comfort of a blue Tibetan cushion, a sheet of plain
paper and a sharpened pencil once made of trees
Our own azure ocean and a paper boat sailing every morning
to the beautiful whatever your words bring me on the breeze.

Rain-topped revelations

And here we are
Again, that time of day
I sit, and unclutter myself of myself
A mug close, cloud-light milk
Steam rising and an ease taking over
My ears loan out their listening to my toes
My eyes, my sight to my skin
My senses, all cloud-light
As you take us on some other adventure
Always the road less travelled
How you seem to find one, every time?
And my fingers move like an octopus with a twitch
Its black ink scrawling across an ocean floor of white
And when you start
I am always the last to know how it will end
But I know when you are close
And relish our little note-booked journeys
So thank you again
For today's rain-topped revelation.

Saying the unsayable

That moment where even words
Perplexed by their own existence
Slide out of themselves
And edge, towards the edge of their page
Only to find no edge, but an ever-stretching expanse
In every direction, fictional and other
Where even a compass with constellations
Won't help them find their way
But where does their writer desire for their travels to take them?

When their every letter, free like a bird
And the paper, a blue sky of wonder, says the unsayable
In every sayable way.

From Jupiter with Love

Much like aligning planets
And with no less precision
Is how
A poem
Comes into being
A celestial alignment of letters and words
An orchestration
Without any conductor
Flitter-flutter islandic thoughts
Submerge, subside
An oceanic peaking

Speaking

Some other language
That finds its worldly place

In the wonder of all things
And in the union of Jupiter, quietude, my pen
And your eyes.

The breaking of bread, the sharing of a poem

A sharing of something from deep within this Earth
Elemental, otherly
Then somehow cohesive
Expansive as it swells in its sustenance
Leavened, light
You might say magical
And the places it reaches
We can feel (and sometimes hear)
But never quite delineate or define

Much like a poem

Arriving from some otherly place
Letters appearing one after the other
A meeting also
Between you and I
Easy on the eye of our hearts
Effortlessly digested
By our yearning appetite for connectedness
And hopefully
Lightly lost, gently so
In the airy leavening that lifts the words
From a page like this, deep into you.

Poems in waiting

Like bread in the oven
Or my morning body pre-yoga
A tightly shut bud
Taking form *sans* quill, ink or parchment
These scribblings making way for verse
They trickle gently and start their flow
In my drafts
Tip-tapped, tap-tipped
All safe
All saved
Before they are sent off into the Universe
To find their adoring eye-catching flight
Comme ça?

The harbour
where all poems sail

Faint as footsteps disappearing
Under the tides of time
My memory sails me back
To the isle
Where we first met
Finding ourselves at each other's horizon
As we watched the leaves of our lives
Take flight
And drift for that first moment
That opened the door
To the depths of eternity
And for something else
To speak
Instead of us
And ever since
Our voices, always second thoughts
Adrift as wavelets
On the very ocean that calculated our meeting
With an infinite precision which now
Captures us into these very lines
And carry us
To the harbour from where all poems sail.

Be my poem?

They asked me
Just like once you did too
"Be my poem?"
"And let me be yours?"

★

This little adventure

Outside my window I can almost see the stars, and inside my body, every organ lets out a yawn

But all I really want is to write and write until these words mingle with other words and together meet their dawn

And you might ask from where do these words come? What lost love, or suffering, or pain made them arrive here on your page?

But I ask you what brought you here? What made us meet like this and led your eyes and my thoughts to in this way engage?

I believe in no coincidences. I am not sure about you, but what meaning do you see in my musings as you hear them echoing inside your head?

After all, we are strangers, you at least know my name and I might never know who you are, nor the past relationships with other writers that you have read

I don't know if you will know my meaning, or paint your own meaning, or perhaps ignore the words and see only the spaces in between

But you were looking for something and somehow you happened across what your eyes see now, and the words that you have already seen

And you are curious and what else might unfold in the rest of this poem. You quickly glance down and see there's still more to read

If we are getting on well, you will smile and say to yourself, "Oh good, there is still more for me on which my eyes can feed!"

And if my thoughts are not quite your cup of tea, you might as well 'jump ship' and give another set a chance

Leaving me in my literal entirety and continuing your search for another writer's more tuneful stance

But if you are still with me, and might I say I am so glad that you are, thank you for letting me share some deep part of myself with you

And how can we call each other strangers anymore? Some part of us just merged and you smile again, as you know this to be true

So here we are sitting on this beautiful planet, hurtling through space, dancing circles around a fireball we call the Sun

And of all the places that we happen to meet, it's like this on these quite lovely pages, and on this little 'book adventure', oh what fun!

2.
Eyes, oh those eyes

An entire chapter dedicated to the eyes. The way they speak for us, always without us knowing. And the ethereal place that gazing with another can carry us both too in those long oceanic dusk-hued swims inside each other's eyes.

Come and dive in, the water's just perfect...

The beautiful tide
of divine possibility

The tide
Between the shores
Of the ports
Of Saying and Unsaying
Is a tide worthy of note
And the message
Even about its existence arrived
One wind-sailed sky day
Brought to me through the wide-open window
That lives wild and true
Between your eyes and mine:

"All that is worthy of being said
Is always left unsaid
Except to the eyes that see the unseen
And all that is seen is said
In the eyes' unsaying
As nothing other than the seen."

When they see, what they see

And I lay my head among
The tiny curls of your hair
Those curls that curve
With the magnificence of mountain clouds
Sailing free with the seasons in tow
Helped by a breeze
As invisible as your kiss
But no less luscious
Than a single tiny dip
Of eyes in eyes
Naked locked lost eyes
Lost with a tender abandonment
But only lost to be found
In the eternity that lives
Always
Beyond what eyes see

When they see
What they see.

Swim-time

Blue
Royal, Prussian
Oceanic, teal
Cadet, aquamarine
Sky-tinted, deep
Ultramarine, navy
Blizzard, pacific
Blue-bell, denim
Cerulean
True

Yes, true
Without opposite
Open, rapturous, inviting

Be it the sea, or the vast sky
That hides secretly for me
In your eyes

I hope that swim-time
Comes around soon some day.

Don't blink?

In a world without echoes
Nor shadows
Nor dawn
Where even time
Isn't able to rust up at its corners

Where the arc of all words
Is always a perfect circle
Made complete
By the bridge of between our eyes
Allowing an exquisite evening dip
Into the untamed majesty
Of wild, notionless beauty
For as long as the bridge allows…

I just have one request
Please don't blink?

Breakfast eyes

Billowing swirls
Always velvety in feel
Elusive to any touch
Mine or yours
Seen somehow without eyes
And not heard with ears
Yet as lovely as any music
Heard always
Inside of our breath's pause
A pause that renders the billowing
And our breath to become one
As surrender comes
And takes all names
Inside the uncloaking
Of that which always was
And is

Meet my eyes again for breakfast
So that we can talk again
Of all this?

Blinks

An ever-present memory
Your eyes, when we first met...

And mine when closed
See them still
Brilliant, piercing
Through my senses
Through time and they still
Suspend me of everything
Just as that day
We met, without meeting
Without being you, or me
When words dared not appear
But we met
In the understanding
That in that one moment of eternity
We had both understood
All there was to ever understand

How wonderful that you still visit me
On the other side of every blink!

Eyes, our eyes

And we sat
Along the banks of our own slumber
You both with the river and without it
And I lost

Studying the waveform
Of your hair

As we sat sipping
Petalled tea
And watched the crowds
Filing back in, before the sun
Found its way back again
And I
Without looking
Escaped
Inside the curvature of each strand
And how they, in unison, undulated their way
Over the vast marine blue that looks into me
And with which I see whenever
I am not looking.

Wild iris

With a blue that belongs
Only to the Earth seen from afar
And to you
With a symmetry I saw borrowed
By all the great places of prayer
Dilating just enough
For me to step in
And lose in the blue hue
Of you
All sense of me.

I hide you

I sit and wait
You, in the midst of your journeying
And wonder
Whether the world notices that I hide you inside my eyes
No matter how far you wander?

A rare shade
of something near to blue

A pigment ever so rarely seen
It caught me, and not just my breath
Unsure how to name it
Closer I ventured, closer still
My heart's lens microscopic
Devouring its play with the light
Angular shelves forging shades anew
Receptive it was
Widening with our intimacy
Until the black abyss of your iris
Pulled me in
And thankfully
Has never let me go.

Free fall

In free fall we are
And everything else too
The moment
The light between
Touches our eyes

As the circuit, now complete
Becomes the key

And us
Lighter than our breath
All density dispersed
Cannot but follow the rapture
And discover the translucency
Outside of our membranes
And want nothing more
Than to stay nestled there
With it, with each other

As nothing but it.

Hold-me eyes

Greyish, calling blues
For years now, the stage of my infinite
Quietly awash, with all that sails
And even the night
That harbours any fragment of me
Hidden under your starry cloak
All to allure my rhythm
To ebb and slow, and at last
To rest
In that mystery that seems to lay
Beyond any dream
And exists in parity
On both sides
Of nothing
But exists somehow (and most of all)

In
Those hold-me eyes...

Form's own ink

Underneath the coat
A surfaceless plane
Vernacular, unhushed
Unnoticed
Except by itself
A seeming impasse to form
But the pigment of form's own ink
And I ask how might they ever meet?
And your eyes tell me everything
Without you telling me anything at all...

Each iris like the Moon

We met
During the Monsoon rains of our time
Ground parched, but magnetic to the heavens
And you spoke
Your words fluttering themselves
On the wings of your breath
And mine
Into the flit-flutter of my heart
Where they again took in the air deep
Before skin diving down between beats
To swim in the realm beneath
Prussian blue currents danced with their midnight
And a quietness, clinging to their feet like weights
They settled in the sands of my ever-deep
And there told me everything you ever wanted to say
And everything I needed to know
But most importantly
You said, "You are my Love."
And I replied, as I always have
With each iris like the Moon.

Eye-lash miles

The long tide-like longing
Like those long
Morning-arm stretching waves
That linger, long and longer still
Magnetic
In their irresistibility
For the uncountable sands
That hold them

Almost as long
As your eyelashes
Yes!

And I haven't even begun to talk about your eyes
We could be here for a while...

Rivulets of time

Rivulets

Flexuous seemingly separate
Though seamlessly entwined, in truth
Yet in this stanza their corpuscles
Very slightly polar in their path
But under the cover of a springtime hush
And the resting acquaintedness
Of a half-moon filled with bluebells
Are written by their writer
Into the centromere of existence
For their thalassic yearning
Cannot but bring them to their sea
Where, upon entering
Their edges melt
And the Universe helplessly follows suit
As the cerulean blue they brought to the sea
Sweeps them up to make a new sky
And scatters their heavenly bodies
An orrery rearranged
And the Moon too, brought into its own plumpness
Fully blossomed and rhapsodic

Another moment being born
From the meeting of thirsty eyes.

3.
Love and other such beautiful truths

What could be more lovely than love? The merging that happens with the other, leading to the disappearance of all centres, all horizons and even all otherness. And perhaps a very similar merging to that we experience when our gaze relaxes in the midst of a beautiful scape of cloud-filled and colour-strewn sky, or as we relax into the toned rhythms of a summering garden.

Inside the so-called ordinary moments that surround us, these and other such beautiful and extraordinary truths await, to pull us in.

Let them and let's see where they take us...

Beauty understood

Bark framed, sanded smooth
A transparent pane, inviting to soothe
With canopied green, filtering the last of the evening light
The warm caress of Summer sitting
Somewhere on a breeze, helplessly admitting
Dancing sounds of birds, to wander carelessly through
And the coalescence of colour that unfolds into view
A shifting scape, reminiscent of a muscular sea
A scintillation, a hovering, leaves swimming upon a tree
The escape of a sigh, beauty understood
Words disperse and disappear, precisely because they should
Leaving the elegance of spoken language
Most responsibly to our eyes
With each to and fro saccade, the moment takes on another guise
Of silkened touch and roaming breath did we become
Kinaesthetic semblance, fusing to succumb
To each other, in each other, like petals of a rose
Lost in the fragrance of a choiceless repose.

Touch softened

Touch softened
Like butter
Making its own way
Through its give
Into a collapse
Of even the subtlest
Of silhouettes
Into dappled light-like
Flutterings, hushings
Enchanted
Notes
Murmurings
Of I don't know what
But interspersions
Of circumnavigations
Butterfly-ed-glances
Whisperings
Nothings
All
Tending
Towards
Where
This line
Leaves you
Now.

Here, there, everywhere, and nowhere

Like an ocean
Resplendent with the patience and wisdom
Of a spring, not waiting for autumn
But knowing
That autumn and spring find themselves in each other
And all seasons and their inbetweening
I settle back into the depths of my roots
And rest
Demagnetised somehow
Untethered, even
From the Moon
As I see the pendulum stop
And pause too
In the centre
Of that which has no centre
And notice as a gentle gale crescendoes across
And sparks of words appear in their own making
Finding their place in the Universe of things
And me both here, there, everywhere and nowhere
Inside and out
As me in you and you in me.

*This beautiful
temple we call Life*

May you sail an emerald sea
Made not of your waiting, nor of your wanting
And be beguiled by your own reflection
In the playground that we together have named sky
May you walk not on this Earth, but with Her
With the bareness of your soles, and bare your soul
If you want to know
The Goddess that you both are
In this beautiful temple we call Life
So that when you bow to Her
With the quietness revealed only to you
In the depths of your awakening
You bow also to yourself
And may the perfume from this secret garden
Linger and accompany
Every escape from your lips
As you see anew the garden's revelations
Blossoming un-shy
With the petal-soft surrender
And beckoning
Of an opening rose
And as step-by-step
You cannot resist
But to move in-step
With Her in-betweenness
And in-touch
With the lightness of how she lives
And loves
Each moment becomes an invitation
To depart the flow of hasty living
And always be arriving at the slow caressed
Cocooning of beingness
That also brings us spring.

Hold me?

A sunset pollen velvet smooth hold
As all-encompassing as the orbits of Neptune and Pluto
Cosier than the unmistakable
Insulating layer of warm sea-like ease
That envelops itself around me in the morning
And our eyes
Locked
Lost
Dilate
As the Universe lapses in concentration
The Earth tilting a little more
With the Moon slowing to watch
And my lines disappear
Spellbound of course, to yours
Folding in and out until they fall free
Even of their DNA pleats
And the only reason that I am left, still held by you
Is because inside this majestic tapestry of cells, seas and stars
Is a single boundless plane-less mirror
That tells me
That
You are my beautiful mystery and that I am yours.

Come get lost?

Come get lost in the oil-black curls of my hair
Let their fragrance, moon-like in intensity
Butterfly-like, in touch
Carry you
And me too
On your own breath (coffee-like)
Through the window
Like the limbus
That sees the truth
Behind the streaming adorning summered golden light
Into the orchestration of everything
Including this meeting
On this particular line
Of our beautifully interwoven existence.

The hidden hush

Caught in the rush
Fingers finding the hidden hush
And a dance made of touch
Sitting in between the glassiness of life
And its sliding doors
Initially revealed with eyes closed
A ballet, more rapturous
Than any thought might think
But this sort of un-dancing
Unseen, to worldly eyes
Finds itself and us
As the only road that beckons us
To one another
As the old, rushed hours
Slowly surrender
To the unhurried
Forever-oasis
That carries
This train
Of words
To
You.

The book of eternity

Your eyes are the question
My hands your gentle, empyreal answer
Your gaze the next sentence
My breath, a tiny little comma
Your hold, the entire paragraph
And more
My smile
The next few
And on we go
Being written into the book of eternity
On the swirling leaves of our lives

But you already knew
And I too
That I am your question wrapped inside your answer
And you my answer wrapped inside my question.

In the shadow of your love

I waited for you to appear
Ever knowing that your orbit would come
Besot me
And take me to the furthest reaches of myself
Where
When I looked carefully enough
I found
Your eyes gazing back
Your words carried by my voice
My touch asleep, inside your skin
My tears, inside your eyes
And only
Our heart at the heart of it all

How could there be any shadowed love
Or indeed my waiting?
When you were here before me
And me before you
And all shadow, but a breath's movement inside
My Love
That is
All you and I.

North of no-where

Still, you live
After months out in-side in-visibility
Here, inside here
So inside that I can't ever find you when I search
Because you live inside the searching
Just north, of no-where
Here, just here
In the gaps between my beats
And over there, across the bluebird sky
In the springtime of all hills
That we call home together
And I call you still mine, and me yours.

Seascape

Briny sprays
Riding above the noisy hushed dispersions
Of the seascape's edge
As it shapes itself
Little by little
A layer breached
A layer beached
Caught in its own sodden sand
There just long enough
To witness that magnetic stretching pull
That thankfully, I know all too well
As the trapped sea breeze bubbles up
Under each resounding watery lapse
That curves back over rocks
And through constellated shingle
Pendular, in its slow dance
Like your breath on my cheek
Reason brimming at its rim
Allowed, a fluid roughened unsteadiness
Yet there, in the midst of its inmost self
A balmy, glassy stillness
From which even the Sun cannot escape
Where the sea and sky's horizon
Reach their ever-present
Dissolving parity
And take us, with them too.

Magnetico

A new word, you say?
No, no, you have tasted its meaning
Close your eyes and let me describe...
It is that feeling that I am close
Even before I come into sight
It is that pull, so deliciously irresistible
That unfailingly, draws me into your arms
It is that inevitability that unfolds into our kiss
When my breath meets yours
It is a word that vanishes itself and us
Into the magnificence of nothingness
Once its work is done.

Falling into Us

As moonlight we were
That night, captured
Outside the vertigo
That catches most
With gravity too having abandoned us
Yet somehow, we were falling
Falling
But what was left to even fall into
Other than falling into us?

Waves

Tip-tap
An ascent of sorts
Angles making way
Corners curved
To the first glimpse
Of the sea
Muscular waves greyed
Silver, azures
I watch for a moment
Before its arms pull me close
Closer than close
Curled and unfurled
With breath
Every inch of me
Flung far outside and in
There, not there
Perhaps there...
Now gone
But wait, there a glimpse
A something
An everything
As we stretch away together
To become the horizon
And cascade our dance
Beyond its edge.

Under the covers

A crowd blurred
Into pulsed passages
Phased, paused, free
Concentric, I wait
In the anticipation of your hush

Steps away, you

Less steps, You

Space between, forgotten
Steps between, lost
We fold in
Under the covers
Of a balmy evening sky
And wander
Through answers, before questions
Never-endings before forever-beginnings
And the us before there was ever
A you or an I.

Braille

My fingers, how they wish to feel and touch

The contours of your face
Smoothened by the winds of time

And to know, without words
Of your moments

And how they long to roam in the curls
Of the waves in your hair

And hold you until our hold
Is all that there is

Like braille to a blindman
How, my Love, you taught me all that I needed to know.

Butterfly heartbeats

Did you know?
That all it takes from you
Is just a glance?
For all my caterpillar heartbeats
To grow wings
And escape the cocoon of my heart
Just to kiss your lips once more?

Meet me?

After midnight, but this side of deep sleep
So that we fall into the deepness together
It's an open invitation
Just for you
And I post it
Via the morse code of the stars
Every night.

The grammar of Love

If breathing
Is made of breath
And kissing
Of kiss
After kiss, after kiss
Does that mean
You
Are made of me?

A PhD in Love

I stopped reading the news
And novels too
The radio waves fall on my deaf ears

And all those letters after my name
Mean nothing to me

For I only want to spend each moment from now
Studying, studying, studying
That which is most important to me
That which makes me feel alive

The one reason my cells came into being
The thousand reasons that I breathe
The ten thousand reasons that the sight of the Moon moves me so
The hundred thousand reasons that allure me into imagining
The thousand thousand reasons that call me to silence
And the thousand to the power of infinity reasons that we met

I just want to know you
Now, to which institution must I apply?

Pre-Love

First, was there the blossoming of dust and light?
Iced into motion, a grand dance
Thawed by a constancy, aglow
And then a torrent
Animated in every way
Seedlings, saplings, the flit-flutter of glass-breath wings
The whispering of the sailing stars
And those whose hearts sailed with them too
Was this the sonata of our life's dawn?

No, no, there was something before

And that something, my Love, was you
That something, my Love, is me and you.

Untitled, but for Rumi

All the little moments of our lives
Sit next to one another in waiting
Wishing it had been them, there
In that moment

Because, my Love, like a little island, I am
Seabound at the thought of our meeting

Fidgeting with an excited innocence
Edging towards the edges of myself
Ready to leap forth
At that first glance into
Into... an... I never remember exactly what
But there, in that fall
Of me into myself and everything into itself
We meet
And talk and hold in the natural way
That the seabed and clouds sleek into their shapes
And listen to the quietest lightening that we have ever heard
And be, just like the midnight sky
As its reflection lies upon quiet waters
And there, just there, you remind me
That we never really meet because we never really parted.

4.
Twenty twenty

I could not write this book, now after the end of 2020, without some reference to the extraordinary events that it brought (and continues to bring). The lockdown imposed solitude of the evenings gave me precious time and space to sit on my blue velvet sofa (as if afloat on the Pacific) and to write.

So, this chapter brings you excerpts from my poetic diary of *Love in the time of Corona*. Musings about everything from my experience of the virus, walking alone on the deserted streets, to the noticing of the extraordinary in the ordinary and, on a more personal note, the tuning into my body asking for yoga and, to my delight, sitting (meditation or yoga meditation, to which I have devoted the chapter after this).

No need to socially distance yourself here, come up close and feel right into them…

Olfactory dullness

Unnoticed in my fretting
Until one morning my coffee
Told me something
That had been there for days
A pronouncement in my throat
Bustling in my nose
And arms and legs saying
Let's not run today
And a head, with a new invisible band
Agreeing, take it easy
Watch the tulips open
The clouds sail by
As the perfume of spring
Passes me by
For now.

Rise

Busy bandwidth lost
All plans deflated
The future is cancelled (was it ever anything else?)
Desires whittled down to the essential basics
Eye contact from distant strangers
And sometimes the neighbour's cat
Learning to bake bread
Instructions over WhatsApp
"Yeast needs warmth and some sweetness
To do its thing."
Distant relatives we must be
Us and yeast?
Yeast lost in the midst of dough
Makes it rise and transcend
Into sustenance, nourishment

What might we do?
If like yeast, we too
Were to help each other rise?

Cessation

The sun falls below
Some far edge
Obscured by suburbia
And the darkening of the sky
Is welcomed by the flickering of screens
Seen through pairs of windows

Yours and mine

Us all living in each other's viewing glasses
Living parallel lives
Across, next to, above and below each other
Busying ourselves within our own radius

Of 10 metres

Ping-ponging if we are lucky enough
From one room to another
And noticing
For
The
First time

The
Cessation
Of time.

Corona walks

New etiquette required
Have you noticed? I'm still learning...
I close the door and scan the road
Decide which side I walk along
Oh, someone approaching
Will they deviate course, or should I?
Ok, my turn it is. I cross, they thank me

In the times of Corona
Pedestrians across the land
Criss-cross their way
On their single socially distant daily
Uber-local micro-adventure
And a new rule for the Highway Code is born:

Number 105 - A new viral etiquette

"Criss-cross as required, telepathy useful but not essential,
body language helpful - early enough for passing (single)
parties to avoid each other's respiratory slip stream and
pass each other safely (min. 2m, if running consider a
greater distance)."

No need to enforce, intuitively understood - our lives are
inter-twined, my health is your health, your health is mine,
my heart is your heart, your heart is mine.

Eye contact

Thoughts circling along with the clouds
I peer out at the trees
And a blackbird bobs by
On my neighbour's roof
Stopping, staring

Ah, eye contact at last

The first and last, beyond a screen, for today
And you know what she told me?
Simply to rest every now and then
Before she bobbed a bit more
And flew away.

New evening routine

No TV at home
YouTube (Yoga with Tim) stretches instead
I undo my lap-topped shoulders
And ease my tense trapezii
As my mind becomes transparent
To today's waves of information
I pick up my downward-dog legs
Stepping out, under the cover of night
I head west
Guided by the light of Venus
Passing trees pregnant with blossom
Sakura cousins maybe? (my exotic imagination...)
And lit by the lamp posts
Lighting the road, just for me
And a cat that crosses over from his house
Thrice this week, to try and greet me
Hoping for a gentle contoured stroke
But since the tiger in Brooklyn turned out to be positive
I have had to decline
The friendly feline
And I continue to step
Towards 10,000
As I make a round, or four
Around Venus and the movie-set roads
Before I head home
To sleep
And wake
And be lucky enough to be able to do it all again.

Tendrils

Strange times we seem to say
"Seasons," might be what the forest whispers
The mystics, "But a portal, a door into yourselves..."
Like tendrils extending out towards us
Probing us, inviting us
To step through
Into the embodied realm
Of our intertwined selves
Tendrils too of this mysterious planetary life.

Running around in circles

Running round in circles
To greet and bid farewell to the day
And in between
What did I do with my precious life?
Too much tip-tapping
(Not so much the poetic sort)
Trying not to take part
In the contagion
Of work-email-anxiety-doing-doing-busying-to-avoid-being
By dropping into a triangle pose
Hoping to find my I
And transform from pose to poise
Poise, inner poise, my fulcrum
For the running of my days.

Zoom yoga

Another day
Back-to-back meetings?

Turn off your camera
Mute yourself and
Listen to the chitter-chatter

Take a deep breath in
Full forwards
Deep breath out
Stretch into the listening
And your breathing
Then slowly unroll up
As the meeting continues to roll on
Hand to your heart
Say Namaste to those online
Shoulders back, hands to the sky and big, graceful arcs
Strong grounded core, feet deep in the earth
And bring your hands back to your sides
Ahhhhh
Feel your inner channels release
And join in the Zoom channel
When you have something to offer
But centred in the quiet, secluded place
That always exists
Between breath and movement
On and off Zoom.

Plain vanilla?

Who would have thought?
That plain vanilla days
Come in such an array of flavours
Blends of mood, longer sleep-ins
Faster morning runs, frothy home-made coffee
'Teams' meetings and the usual
"You're on mute!"
Under-whelming government policy
(At least they're consistent)
Computer crashing twice
Trying to eat well
A Vinyasa or 12, evening walks
Just to see the gorgeous full Moon
Calls with parents
Roots growing out
And
Then
I
Suddenly
Thought
Did I not even wear a bra today?
No one would have noticed in this 2D life!

Pink Moon gazing

Gazing into another's soul
A recognition of each other
In the eyes across the airs
But the streets like a movie set
Picture perfect, lit
Deserted
Lights on and everyone home
Traffic lights changing, no one waiting
All quiet, all still
Just the Pink Moon and me
And I look up
And see her gazing down

Ah, at last someone to gaze at
In this lone-island phase
Of our Venus and moon-scaped lives.

Surya '0830' Namaskar

A spinal welcome to the fresh morning air

C1 to L5 and all before 9

My vertebrae crackle and click

For them relief

Paravertebral muscles awakened

A conference ensues

A concert in fact

The conductor, my long moonbeam breaths

As my body re-learns to move with the ease and grace

Of a feline, or

An ocean stretching out on to shore

Long crested stretches

Ah, and a release

The poses of Surya Namaskar

My gateway

To nowhere at all

Other than to myself

And all before 9.

Homage

To what or to whom?
But that is what running is
Just after dawn
Alone, yet not
Before I give myself to my day
Running gives itself to me

Symmetric, rhythmic breathing
My new compass
Limbs like a locomotive
They follow the steaming from my lungs
Until running becomes a train ride
A journey and me the comfy passenger
Not even noticing the soft rain
As the scape escapes
And somehow, without really thinking
I always arrive back at the same station
Home
From my homage to me
And to the quietly lived streets
To being able to be met by the Earth
Step after step
And my homage to my limbs and feet
And to my shoelaces (that I double tie)
And of course my most faithful companion on these runs
My beloved trainers
Thank you for my (almost) daily homage
Outside and in.

Astronaut home-visits and tea

The excitement of being able to commute
Not just from my bedroom to the study
But outside, on the roads
Just me, my breath and my cycle
Some suburban navigation, then an expanse of green
Blackheath – named at the time of another plague
Then the tree-lined avenue in Greenwich Park
With the now empty sky-scrappers at its pinnacle
But I take a left and freewheel down
You all know that taste of freedom
And eventually I arrive at the surgery

Quiet again
Because people are too scared to contact us
And we grow ever scared
Of what is happening to them at home

But then the highlight of my day
My favourite and most glamorous patient
75 years, forever young
But with not long left
A visit to her home
Her hair still salon-styled
Warm, welcoming eyes
And I bet
Her usual red-lippy beneath her mask
And me looking like a bedraggled astronaut
My sauna suit she calls it – which makes me laugh
And we chat and she giggles
As my suit squeaks as I bend down to examine her feet
And she sweetly offers me apple crumble
And what turned out to be our farewell tea.

Little miracles

That previously never came to my attention (not exhaustive):

1. Post, hand-delivered, to my door. From anywhere on this planet
2. Mirrored smiles, with strangers
3. The loveliness of gazing (now a distant memory, although Zoom isn't bad)
4. Honey and the evening light being first cousins
5. Tulips – the flowers and what your mouth has to do to make the sound of the word tulip!
6. Strawberries from Spain. Still? (We are in a pandemic…)
7. The milk-tray man antics of the squirrel that sits at the top of my tree
8. The delicious hypnotic depths of deep sleep that continue to find me – thank you!
9. Bulbs bursting through with Gauguin colours
10. And every precise, slow, deliberate, delicate, space-allowing, all-stretching, body-yawning, elemental vertebral movement of a beautiful little Vinyasa flow - thanks to Yoga with Tim & Adrienne.

Power

(Written during the 1st Covid wave in London, May 2020)

8 weeks
Of working in leggings
No ironing (what joy!)
Making friends with the cashier in Tesco
But not getting too close
Watching the tree outside my study
Spring into spring, day by day
Watching the scales in my bathroom
Hmmm... day by day
Getting my smiles
More from my mirror and Zoom
The largest expanse of cycle-under-me-sky
That I have ever known
Each day an invitation to feel the wind under my helmet
And my limbs rhythmically follow my breath
But instead, I choose running
It's definitely more mind than legs
Although there are days that running chooses me
And each passing day
At the 5pm broadcast
I realise

That neither integrity nor competence are a pre-requisite
For
Power or
Position

And knowing this is Your Power and Mine.

The velocity of hope

The velocity of hope
And of love
Bear the same trajectory
And can outmanoeuvre
Even the stealthiest of things
And do you know why?

Because both hope and love
Live here
Where we do too

On this side of all distance
And outside of time
Even the universal laws of physics
Gave up
Trying to apply themselves.

Summertime living, anytime living

1. Leave an open window at night, between you and the Moon

2. Make sure you allow your whole skin to feel the sun and bathe in the bath of meditation, at least once a day

3. Walk and watch the birds cutting the air on their own skywalks

4. Stretch your body and await the release and melting of dense areas

5. Nourish your heart (conversation and tenderness when permissible) and your body (yes, chocolate does count)

6. Water your soul

7. Take a blank sheet of white paper and see where your pencil sails you

8. Rest your eyes in green, more than just once

9. And most definitely make place and space, to do nothing *sans* guilt

10. Ease with ease, into and out of your day.

The deadliest of moments

The deadliest of moments
Are those when we forget to live
When we lose the ability to be arrested
By the wondrous layers of blossom on a branch
Reaching out to you
Reminding you
Pink paper-thin petals propelling themselves
Out of the sleek barked branches
What sort of miracle is this?
What sort of miracles are these? And every springtime?
So next time your stride is hurried
Trying to reach somewhere, a little faster
Allow the little miracles of life to meet you, here
Where you always are
In between strides
Living the true moments
Of your own miraculous life.

The loveliness of lettuce

The give of a tomato
Light playing on the contours
Of cucumber
Greek sun released in crumbling feta
All laced in Tuscan liquid gold
And a pizzazzy handsome balsamico
Dressed with seeds (seeds!)

Why did it take me 43 years to notice
The wonders of this beautiful, simple life?

Contagion

There are still things
More contagious than Covid
Smiles, kindness and love.

Colander living

This new simple life
A colander of time and space
Filtering
Only what's really important.

Love lightly

Like the moment just before a kiss
Or the blink before our eyes meet
A little like after our touch disappears into itself
Or the unnumbered, unencumbered seconds
That hang lightly between
Turning from the last page, to this
To meet these letters assembled
Calling you to love lightly
Me, and more than me, You.

5.
Dates at eight

In 2020, we were all invited to find our saving grace – safe harbours and sheltered bays, offering moments of nestled, *cutched up* rest (*cutch*, or *cwtch* in Welsh, means all snuggled up) and perhaps also something deeper.

For me, grace came along in the form of sangha and of sitting (meditation) with *Francis*, every night at 8pm GMT. Me on my blue velvet sofa, under a cloud-white blanket, eyes-closed journeys never knowing where they will lead, and always without going anywhere at all.

My dates at eight continue to introduce me to the solace that lives in my own depths, and not because of what I hold on to, but of what each night I let go of.

And they also led me to these poems about sitting, *a Lovers' conversation of sorts*. So, come and sit with me too?

Ton cœur, l'invitation

Another date at eight
Ton cœur, l'invitation
Et j'accepte toujours
De se baigner, ensemble
In the pool
Not so hidden, in fact
Made
Of an utterly delicious somethingness
With wells of echoing silence
And no shores to enclose it
For it needs no embrace
As I take a dip
Dans ses ondulations
Et sa caresse me déshabille
As I fall
Into being
Like water
Avec elle-même
Gentle warm waves of surrender
Unorchestrated ripplings
Blurring, softenings, dissolving happenings
Dissolvingly watching
As my breath takes flight, like a winged bird of paradise
Flying free, gracious in her strokes
And what is left
Est seulement nous.

Scintilla

Scintilla
Dots
Brownian
In their motion
Breath-like
In their notion
Lifted, afloat
Half-asleep, sweetly drunk
On their own twilight
Dissolving, resolving
A question
Evolving
Into its own
Awakened answer
Scintillating
Still
A near-distant star
Morse-code pulses
That only
You
Can know
As
Me
Saying, "Yes!"

This quietly
come-hither weave

A gossameric weave
Like birds in the sky
Sometimes curving lines
Other times simple dots
Vanishing
And with eyes closed too
My own curves
Reduce themselves
Down
To their bare threads
So fine, thinned ever more
With and without understanding
Until I am invited
Somehow
Beyond
My very own vanishing
And am left
Naked
In the midst of this
Quietly come-hither
Weave.

The breath of Aphrodite

Mid-week
My date at eight
Shutters slow to close
As I allow the day's agenda to leave me
And
Settling in
My body melts and merges
With the blue velvet of my chair
Inviting it
To grow mysterious mycelia through my porous skin
Into me
And the moment moulds me and it
Softening our angles
Feathering them to a cloud-like lightness
Maybe even more faint
Like some mid-distance star
Perhaps there, perhaps not, no one can ever be quite sure
And then a sea breeze obeying the Moon's whispers...
Amplitudes of slow waves, slow rise, slow fall
Yet far more expansive than my old breadth
The breath of Aphrodite herself, breathing into me
Until my skin surrenders, all gates opened
Succumbing, transparent from her charms
And naked of everything
Except the beauty
Of what she reveals
As this
Little
Moment
Itself.

Another eyes-closed journey

Another eyes-closed journey
Destination never known
Because in fact I never go anywhere
But inside, through the secret door
On the other side of movement
As I slide into a comfy warm armchair
From where I watch
My body fade into the eyes-closed night
And settle beneath the sway of swaying breath
As it blinks back a little from here and there
Free of any silhouette or mapped constellation
Like a true starry night
Then a story, like a comet, appears
Leaving its evanescent trail of thought

Ordinarily I would try and hitch a ride
But I am slowly growing used to just watching
Acrobatics and beautiful synchronizations
Finding more and more
Their own resolution
And sometimes I drop off
Into a little dreamtime
A tender, sweet reminder
Inside the reminder
All whilst
Sitting
Eyes-closed here.

See-saw sitting

Sitting on my velvet blue sofa
I am a little rowing boat
Of sitting
With eyes closed
Though a sinking
Just under the white-noised chitter-chatter of life
Where thoughts and clouds mingle and melt
And breath too, autonomous
Is seen
My heart becomes like a raindrop
Rippling in a pond
And I watch as I un-cling from myself
Letting go somehow, of my own supposed sails
Watching a quiet breeze of gentle dissolution
Of all and anything I called Me
And it is precisely at this moment
That I start to see
From a never-ending scape
Where somehow
There is nothing that is not me.

Water's edge

Why are we so beckoned?
To this
Some stark fluid fault of experience
There at the edge of something
Peering in
Always
To find us peering back
One foot
On what holds us
The other's toes cooed into curiosity
At a threshold
This nexus of two scapes

Is it because we too are mostly water?
With a dash of soil and a hint of Jupiter?

And standing at the water's edge
We speak, but not with words
And not with me

And the nexus of two scapes
Gives way to the nexus of all scapes
And all escapes

Outside of all edges
Simply standing
At the water's edge.

Bumble bee meditation

Like a pair of bumble bees
The yellow velvet chairs sit together in my house
Always happy to accommodate
My weighty yet ephemeral movements
Patiently they hold me
And whatever I cling to that day
Their buttery yellow warmth
And my contours eventually
Melt
Open and the entire sky comes in
Thoughts and their cousins now lift like paper-light kites
Ever long lines
But no anchor to be found
And off they go
(And they might well return too)
Leaving me exactly where and as I left myself
Before I forgot that I was ever here.

My own Shakti

No blue velvet sofa
Instead, metallic teal
At the edge of my garden
I peer in
Past the planted pots
Pots sowed with seeds and a little hope
Hoping for inspiration from a passing bee
Or bird song
As I look at the eight-armed Laurel tree
Standing at the head of my little oasis
The Shakti of my oasis
Lithe, strong and elegant
With a wild ease
Perfect poise
Reminding me
To be the Shakti
Of my own inner oasis.

Dates at eight

Dates at eight
A velvet ocean chair
My date at eight
With sitting (and You)
As the night slides in, and my eyes close
Weather and thoughts mingle
Enjoying a little, light conversation
And a not-so-secret door
Opens
A defocusing
A sinking back, a slinking back
Beyond seeing
Yet seeing
Dispersions
Dissolving
Ever fraying and ever free
Something splaying, invisible-stretching
My body, gossameric
Now constellatory
Like stars
Scintillating, a quiet ember
Blinking away and back in
All the secrets of the Universe
Afloat yet dancing a quantum dance
To the very music that sees them into their being
And sings us, too, into a melody
Where we meet and watch ourselves
As the music, that somersaults
Over itself
Again
And again
And again.

The ocean herself

Winter walking down the path
The blind of night, darkening
A little further
Into the day
But now, it's almost eight
And my date
With sitting and watching
The inside workings of every clock
Stop
At a little after
As my own blinds shut
And I settle slow
Listening to a voice, afar
Yet as close as my own breath
As faraway tides settle into sands on their furthest reach
And stars emit their effortless faraway light
I too surrender
Unclip, unfasten
And slip in, through the gap
To slip out and out further
Capacious, unending rippleless rippling
All here
Sailing free without any boat
But simply
As the beauty
Of the ocean herself.

The blackbird
of Kashmiri Tantra

I sit
Waiting for the words to find me
In the distance, a blackbird
I wonder
Are you the first words?
And I wait
For I have learned to wait
It wasn't the blackbird after all
It was these...
The trembling in my chest mimicking springtime leaves
And billowing densities of sensation
Roaming freely through my torso
The diaphragm no barrier to them
And then a settling in my throat
Like clouds nestling themselves in a valley
And I sit, and watch and wait
And like that blackbird I leave my perch, curious
To venture towards these new visitations
Greeting them, upon meeting them
I dive in and circle again and again
Never finding their centre, nor any edge
And in fact I never find anything there, and yet they remain
Subtle visitors from beyond
And as I learn to release
My resistance towards them
My blackbird of Kashmiri Tantra
Vanishes
And I find myself as all that I behold
Including these divine visitations
That chose this moment to dance.

This day-like dream

Technical problems
No impulse to change
My eyes close
Another delicious date at eight
I dive in and straddle the water gently
And then you dive in too
A welcoming
Of all and every current
My skin serene and silent
And deeply
Asleep
My breath at all stretch
As little by little
I let go of all notes
Of all sailing shadows
And watch the current of air
Come
And leave
As slowly
I drop
Deep
Into that place
Of cushioned
Comfy nestling
Delicious cloud-like afloatness
Undisturbed
Unperturbed
Until I venture
Back into this day-like dream.

Black hole meditation

Black hole meditation
Eight on the clock of now
A blue velvet sofa
Instead of legs crossed
And a blanket of waved cotton
With me underneath
Concepts parked on some double line
Never were they a problem
As a thought or two skips by
And sounds too
In some sort of Brownian motion
Unable to converse in the language of now
Nebulous shifting sensations
Some vying for my eyes
The bare bones of beingness
Appearing
In my seeing
Somehow with me mixed in
And not
With them and you
And the vast expanse of plain sailing silence
That vanishes us at eight
And dropped us off
Here.

The sea is me, the sea is you

The sea is me, the sea is you
Blue velvet beckoning
A blanket to match
I slip under
To sit
My Saturday patiently waits
As I sink back
As far and deep
As is humanly possible
And watch as my body becomes
Like a current in the sea
Embraced along
With all that passes by
Whispering in its essence
Unpredictable in its touch
Slowly melodious
In its movement
But always
In the sea that is me
And the sea that is you.

Yogini Goddess

You search for this Yogini Goddess, Pearl Oyster High Queen
The One who wears your breath, naked Majesty unseen?

She, who, with the slightest glance of eternity does will
Every heavenly body to move and orbit with divine precision
and skill

She births the laws of physics in every moment that charm
quanta, cell and moon
To waltz the tides of all oceans and quickstep every summer
monsoon

Your eyes and these words wouldn't be meeting were it not
for her thought's gaze
Such is her Grace and Beauty and the Intelligence of her ways

And every look of Love is her calling, is a falling into her eyes
Where unbeknownst to you, she undresses you of all of your
imagined guise

And here with words unneeded, her eyes magnetic tell you
of nothing and all
Why search for the Yogini Goddess when she dwells deep
within, just follow her silent call.

The Lovers' conversation

On all sides of the Ocean
And in the waves between that reveal
A never-ending Lovers' conversation
Inked in sea-breeze kissed teal

And in salt-crystalled zephyrs singing
To a chorus of migrating birds
The answer to your every question
Hidden among these words

Oh beautiful searching eyes of wonder
What possibly could I intend?
Why, this unexpected soirée - just You and I
And this moment that together we spend

Upon these words, a little poem bridge
Between your eyes and my heart and my hands
An encounter made possible only from beyond
For we dream our dream from different lands

So may I please tell you of the Lovers' conversation?
Of which the zephyrs sing to the yearning skies
Close your eyes, just for moment, and watch
As your breath by itself does gently fall and rise

And allow the zephyrs' song to touch and dissolve you
No body, just currents mingling in a serene sea
Where all your questions will find their eternal answer
If you become too the Lovers' conversation with me.

6.
Leave space for Ireland too?

This chapter is a late, but meant to be addition (*I have mentioned before that with poems, I am the last to know, but it seems now that this is the case with entire chapters too*), and this is how she came into being, and into being here with you…

I have been charmed by the thought of the Emerald Isle for some time and with a name derived from the Old Irish word for Goddess, Ériu, how could anyone not? But then I happened across the enchanting poetry of David Whyte, who speaks of her quiet grace and wild, rugged beauty. As did his close friend, Irish poet John O'Donohue.

While planning a visit to Connemara in August 2021, a friend asked me about this book, to which I replied, "Well, after months and months she is finally there." And then he so wisely said to me, *"Perhaps leave space for Ireland too?"*

And so, here we are…

Ta me ag súil le

(As close to the word 'expectations' as we can get in the beautiful Irish language. The direct translation is 'that I am looking forward to'. And a note of thanks to KM and his neighbour for this and the other Irish language translations.)

Raw, wild calling Irish beauty
Framing clouds, rumpled grey
Pearly slate, oyster sitting
Above long-travelled waters breaking
Moon-timed waters making
An abundance of fresh salt-laden mist
Unweighted and unwaiting
For this Goddess knows no difference
My cheeks, your lips or verdant, run-away hills
Grass adorned with light like Indian gold
Trembling in the Atlantic's breath
Wholesome but strong in will
And carrying a song to beckon you still
Come and find this place with me?

This place where
Is ceol mo chroí thú[1]
And I am the music of yours
You get there by the road called Sky[2].

---

[1] *Is ceol mo chroí thú* – Irish for 'You are the music of my heart'.
[2] Referring to the Sky Road, Clifden, Connemara.

Comhráite fíor

(Irish for 'truthful conversations')

The place of longing
And belonging
Is a place
We all know well
And in Ireland
She has a name
And you will know her
When you travel there and meet her
For she wears the most viridescent of greens, all lush
Quietly singing among the hush
Of heather - crimson, persian red or indian pink
And her
Sitting
At the edge, of all edges
Where two bodies first meet
The muscular sea
Who shapes her every shore, beach and lip
And her, the land, blessed emeraldine
Ériu her Goddess name
And here, *on this very inconstant line*
Is where
The truthful conversation at last begins.

St Oran's?
Or some place else?

A coalescence
A welling up
Unclear
From which precise spring
Nor when, nor why
But beautifully unencumbered
And untrammelled too
Cursive, in how its story
Is written
Into being
Fluent
In every language
Most especially, that of the eyes
As exquisitely balanced
As it is
Magnetically charmed
As glimpse, after glimpse
Of its healing waters
Invites from within us
The courage to hold close
The most distant of our own horizons
And that which lies too
Beyond our vanishing point
All within
Our very own entirety

Take a dip with me
Let's see for ourselves?

Secret doorway

Quite by itself
It arrives
That call
To fall
And unbeknownst quite how
Or why
But with the most diaphanous
Of announcements
It appears
Out of nowhere
But with an allure
That even a Magnetar
Couldn't rival
And
In the midst
Of all the bustle
The Universe can rustle
Chit-chatter, porridge by the park
Or oysters, revolving waiters and clinking glass
It still manages to arrive
With the same mingling
Of breath, meeting breath
That call, to fall
Through the secret doorway
Of your eyes and mine.

Divine benefactions

An idyllic odyssey
From beyond
The edge of the ocean
Back, almost
To the mouth of the sea
We arrived, *back into* time
As the clock struck four

At the hearth of this city
The line, long
But met, we were
By mirrored patience and warmth
More than an ember
Glowing, growing
As we sat together
Sharing and slowly sipping tea
Our words, companionate
Of single origin too
As the waters of accustomed conversation
Gently parted to reveal
A divine, sweet indulgence
Afferent
And not of our knowing
All sustenance and nourishment
Healing too
As hallowed words appeared
And made light
That which was always made of light
And of Love
Unstainable by any glass
Birthed of a Purity of Spirit
Those who know would say
And served, on this delightful occasion
With a slice of cake
And a cup of tea.

A tonic for the soul

Tonics in life
Come in a variety of guises
And from the island of Ireland
Here are a few:

Bare feet on lush, moist, velvety greens
Warm smiles on every street
Magnetic walks everywhere we went
Harmonious chatter, always in tow
A library, nothing short of the Divine
And more worthy than any altar
Where all words surrender by themselves
Enveloped
Cocooned dinners, in the midst of the stir

A landscape calling
On the Western side
She called first to you
And through you, me too

Modest, restrained beauty
Gentle undulating hills
Hidden coved beaches
Sand, powder soft
Land nestled close with sea
Breath-slow, closed-eye walks
Under shushing leaves
Poetic
In every way

But it always was (and thankfully still is)
Those moments
That *catch us* in their breath, whenever we gaze
And don't easily let us go, on this island
Made only of Us.

Somersaulting time

It must be so
Because
You were there with me
In that past
That is now
As uncertain as the future
But who was really there?
When we both know
That you were there in your own absence
And I too, in mine
Which of course, is why we really met…
And travelled so
Without really travelling anywhere
At all.

The doors of Dublin

Wrought iron
Gilded gold
By eyes that see
Sunrise shaped
Fanlight crowns
Adorning
Grand, broad oaked faces
Glass tempered hearts
Ornate, embellished
Art-deco, Prismatic

Irised

A kaleidoscope of colour
Cerise, magenta
Goddess Ériu's emerald chartreuse
Greek Temple-esque pillars
Handsome Georgian
Redbrick frames

But

Symmetrical in their affection
And in all lines of their infinite perfection
These doors
Altars to beauty
The Irish say
"Enchanted entryways
To the Otherworld..."

Wait for me on the other side?

The promise of the sea

In search of the
Hidden coves of longing
We were
Until this particular journey
Called
And promised us
The sea
And like all our journeys
Together
Of getting lost
And found
In each other
With time in past tense
The promise
Circled us back
To the point
At which we both stood
And still stand
A point with no centre
And an ever-gazing expanse
With no horizon
Where distance too is past
And
Where the sea and sands of longing
Merge and become
Those not just of belonging
But also, of beholding
Inside us now
As
The promise of the sea.

Connemara's blessings

Being invited to witness
The marriage of the holy wilding waters
Of the Atlantic
And the body divine
Of the Irish coast
Is
One of the holiest
Of this isle's many hidden blessings
And an open invitation
To those who see
Even when walking
With eyes-closed
The gifts hidden in plain sight
Of
The lightness of their being
And the beautiful blur
Of this one
Brush of beauty
Untamed
Unnamed
All living lines betrothed
To the farthest most points
Yet even to be birthed into view
Where all clouded veils are lifted
And where the wise sky gives us her name too.

Friday evening drinks

A thin slice
Of infinitely precise
Geographical
Time
Or so it seemed...
Served over
A rather sensational stir
Akin
Somehow to a quiet
Butterfly-winged whirr
Anticipation, not so hidden…
Found right there
Free, unshy
Dancing
In the midst of irises
Locked, unlocked
And something
Sweet-bodied
Expanding
Beyond the seconds and minutes
And dilating irises too

As we watched *and* listened
To ourselves
Inside and outside
Our conversation

And all this
Over
Friday evening drinks.

Connemara midnight blue

There I lay
My body afloat under the covers
Between the worlds of day and dream
My thoughts like fisherwomen and men
Throwing out their long lines
Mine baited with the words
That had washed up on my shore
Unplanned, by design, only the sea's currents knew
And ever know...
And I wait
Hovering, without waiting
Enjoying the gentle glide towards sleep
But then
Out of the language of the midnight blue
Which you know too - it's the same
That met our feet in Connemara
On that open, sandy bay
Came two or three little suggestions
And my thoughts gently
Pulled them in close
Yes!
They work, perfectly!
All I need to do now is remember...
And that's the last thing that I remember!

Of my almost dream-time
Midnight escapade
My words swimming free
Like they always did, and do
Just like me and you
But unlike them
We know too
To be the sea
The sea that is you
The sea that is me.

7.
Paper boat sailing –
your turn now...

Where have the words and spaces that filled the pages before taken you? A few pages of perfect calm seas now await, with just the right amount of wind for you to sail, with your own thoughts, free on your own paper boat.

Let's see where you take me...

Afternoon tea anyone?

We sat, on opposite sides
Normally our feet
Would take care of the talking
But this time
Somehow it was our eyes
Both resting upon one another
But also, within a trinity of being(s)
Accompanied too with lush cake and tea
Sweetened with more than a dash of conversation
And I remember being asked
About the first book

'What is its name?', he said
'Fall in love with Love with me?', I replied
Beaming, 'Little l love for the first, and big L Love for the
second...'
'Ah,' he said as his eyes understood, 'What an invitation?'

And at this point I had no idea
How ready my cells were
To abandon me
Disrobing themselves faster than light
Sliding invisibly
Outside of their own membranes
Cytoplasms running free
Into You!
As you replied, 'Yes, so I did...'

And that, Dear Reader, or Fellow Poet I should say
Was the last I ever saw of me!

I so hope that you too
Lost yourself a little in these pages
And in their calling spaces?

Another little note

To all of you who have encouraged me in my poetic wonderings and wanderings – *thank you*. Especially those of you at Rupert's retreats who so generously helped me to nurture my heart and my voice, and where year after year, you gazed and listened whilst I recited, and helped me become ever brave in sharing even the most revealing and intimate of my poems.

To Rupert, for showing me all those years ago, that writing poetry is *my sadhana*. *To Michael and to Thomas*, for both encouraging me in *my writing* and in *my sitting*. *To Raficq, for all our poetic exchanges, they remain a beautiful dream. And to Jenny and Richard* for helping me to share these *Birds of Love* and for delighting in them. *Merci à tous.*

To you, Dear Reader of my oasis thoughts – thank you. I hope these poems, like any good journey, have taken you somewhere new within yourself. And if they have, I would love to hear back, so please do write and let me know?

And finally, to Mash and Veronica – thank you. Without you this book wouldn't be as beautiful as she is.

Rachna xx

London, December 2020 – which somehow stretched its way into March 2022 – I mentioned before, I am always the last to know...

About the author

Rachna Chowla is a doctor by day and a poet by night, a poet/publisher to be more precise. This is her second collection of poetry. Her first collection *'Fall in love with Love with me?'* was published in 2017 and was the reason that she started The Swirling Leaf Press.

Since then, the Press has helped other poets and non-fiction writers share their work. The Swirling Leaf Press has only one requirement – that their writing in some way expresses *Love, Truth & Beauty.*

"Like birds coming to a drinking pool, the poems arrive. They decide all structure and all form, and I read as they write themselves onto my page. And the more I write, the more I feel that words will never be able to completely describe the mystery from where they come, these beautiful poem-bird teachers of mine.

Thank you for allowing me to share them with you, because as I hope you now see, they so gracefully share themselves with me."

Made in the USA
Las Vegas, NV
31 July 2022

52460122R00142